THE GREAT BOOK OF JORDAN FACTS

AN EDUCATIONAL COUNTRY TRAVEL PICTURE BOOK FOR KIDS ABOUT HISTORY, DESTINATION PLACES, ANIMALS AND MANY MORE

Copyright @2023 James K. Mahi

Jordan is **located in the Middle East,** bordered by Syria to the north, Iraq to the northeast, Saudi Arabia to the south, and Israel and Palestine to the west.

What is the national animal of the jordan?

National animal: The Arabian oryx native to desert and steppe areas of the Arabian peninsula.

What is the national bird of the jordan?

National bird: The Sinai rosefinch is a small songbird with a pink body and black head. It is found in the deserts of Jordan, Israel, and Egypt.

What is the national sport of the jordan?

Football (soccer) is the most popular sport in Jordan.

What is the national tree of the jordan?

The Quercus ithaburensis Decne. or Quercus aegilops, also known as the Palestinian oak, is the national tree of Jordan.

What is the official name of the Jordan?

Official name: The Hashemite Kingdom of Jordan

What are the people of the Jordan called?

People: Jordanians

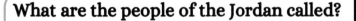

How big is the Jordan?

The area of Jordan is **89,342 square kilometers (34,495 square miles).** It is about the size of Indiana.

Which city is the largest in the Jordan ?

Largest city: Amman

What is the population of Jordan ?

Population: About 10 million people

Is the Jordan overly populated?

Overpopulated? No, Jordan is not overly populated.

How many provinces does the Jordan have?

Provinces: Jordan is divided into **12 provinces.**

What percentage of the Jordan covered by rainforests?

Rainforests: Only about 0.1% of Jordan is covered by rainforests.

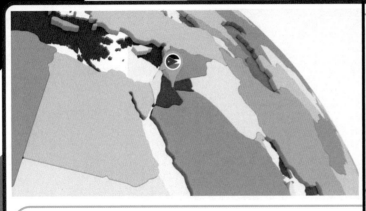

What percentage of the world's land does the Jordan occupy?

Percentage of the world's land: **Jordan occupies about 0.3%** of the world's land.

How many time zones are there in the Jordan ?

Time zones: **Jordan is in two time zones, UTC+2 and UTC+3.**

What is Jordan nickname?

Nickname: **The Hashemite Kingdom**

Who ruled Jordan first?

First ruler: **The first ruler of Jordan was the Emir Abdullah I**, who ruled from 1921 to 1951.

What is the oldest city in Jordan ?

Oldest city: The oldest city in Jordan is **Amman**, which has been continuously inhabited for over 7,000 years.

What is the highest temperature ever recorded in the Jordan ?

Highest temperature ever recorded: The highest temperature ever recorded in Jordan was **54°C (129°F) in 1942.**

What is the lowest temperature ever recorded in the Jordan ?

Lowest temperature ever recorded: The lowest temperature ever recorded in Jordan was **-13°C (8°F) in 1992.**

Which months are the coldest in the Jordan ?

Coldest months: The coldest months in Jordan are December, January, and February.

Which months are the hottest in the Jordan ?

Hottest months: The hottest months in Jordan are July and August.

What was the old name of the Jordan ?

Old name: The old name of Jordan was Transjordan.

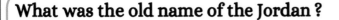

What is the most famous tourist destination in Jordan?

The most famous tourist destination in Jordan is **Petra**, an ancient city carved into the rocks.

What are some of the interesting things to see and do in Jordan?

Some of the interesting things to see and do in Jordan include visiting Petra, hiking in the Wadi Rum desert, swimming in the Dead Sea, and exploring the Roman ruins of Jerash.

The capital city of Jordan is Amman, which is also the largest city in the country.

Arabic is the official language of Jordan.

Jordan is known for its rich history and archaeological sites. **The ancient city of Petra, a UNESCO World Heritage Site,** is one of the most famous tourist attractions in the country.

The Dead Sea, located in Jordan, is **the lowest point on Earth and known for its high salt concentration**, allowing people to float effortlessly on its surface.

The Dead Sea is 423 meters (1,382 feet) below sea level.

Jordan has a diverse landscape that includes deserts, mountains, and the fertile Jordan Valley.

The **national flag of Jordan** features three horizontal stripes of black, white, and green with a red triangle on the hoist side, and a seven-pointed star in the center of the triangle.

Jordan is a constitutional monarchy, with King Abdullah II as the current monarch.

The official currency of Jordan is **the Jordanian Dinar (JOD).**

Jordan is known for its **hospitality and welcoming culture.** Guests are often greeted with coffee and dates, which are traditional symbols of hospitality.

The cuisine of Jordan includes dishes such as Mansaf (a traditional Bedouin dish), **Falafel, Hummus, and Maqluba** (a layered rice and meat dish).

The national dance of Jordan is called the "Dabke." It is a traditional folk dance performed in a group, usually during celebrations and weddings.

The official religion of Jordan is Islam, and the majority of Jordanians are Muslims.

Jordan is home to several nature reserves, including the Dana Biosphere Reserve and Wadi Rum, which is famous for its stunning desert landscapes.

Jordan has a high literacy rate, with education being highly valued in the country.

The economy of Jordan is based on industries such as tourism, pharmaceuticals, agriculture, and mining.

The official national holiday in Jordan is Independence Day, celebrated on May 25th, commemorating the country's independence from British mandate rule in 1946.

Jordan has a moderate climate, with hot summers and cool winters, but temperatures can vary depending on the region.

The famous movie "Lawrence of Arabia" was filmed partly in Jordan's Wadi Rum desert.

Mount Nebo is an important religious site in Jordan, believed to be the place where Moses saw the Promised Land before he died.

The Jordanian desert is home to several Bedouin communities who have a nomadic lifestyle.

Jordan has a rich tradition of handicrafts, including pottery, mosaics, and traditional textiles.

Jordan is known for its traditional music, which often incorporates instruments such as the oud (a stringed instrument), flute, and drums.

The city of Aqaba, located on the Red Sea coast, is a popular destination for diving enthusiasts, thanks to its vibrant coral reefs.

Jordan is home to the lowest golf course in the world, called the Ayla Oasis Golf Course, situated near the Dead Sea.

The official national flower of Jordan is the black iris, which is found in abundance in the country's nature reserves.

The ancient city of Petra was designated as one of the New Seven Wonders of the World in 2007.

Only 15% of Petra has been explored. This means that there are still many secrets to be discovered in this ancient city.

Jordan has several natural hot springs, including the Ma'in Hot Springs, where visitors can relax and enjoy the therapeutic waters.

There are over 100,000 archaeological sites in Jordan. This makes it one of the most important archaeological sites in the world.

Jordan is a safe and stable country. It is a great place to visit for families and solo travelers alike.

- The Dead Sea Scrolls, ancient religious texts discovered in the 1940s, were found in the vicinity of the Dead Sea in Jordan.
- Jordan is known for its traditional festivals and celebrations, such as the Jerash Festival, the Al-Balad Music Festival, and the Arab Wedding Festival.
- The "Jordan Trail" is a long-distance hiking trail that spans the entire country, offering stunning views of Jordan's diverse landscapes.
- The national sport of Jordan is football (soccer), and the country has its own professional football league.
- Jordan has a rich history of soap-making, with the city of Nablus being famous for its traditional olive oil soap production.
- The ruins of the ancient city of Umm Qais, located in the north of Jordan, offer panoramic views of the Sea of Galilee and the Golan Heights.
- The city of Madaba is known for its ancient mosaic map of the Holy Land, dating back to the 6th century AD.
- Jordan has several natural reserves dedicated to the protection of wildlife, such as the Shaumari Wildlife Reserve, where endangered species like the Arabian oryx and Persian onager are bred.
- Jordan has been a filming location for numerous Hollywood movies, including "Indiana Jones and the Last Crusade" and "Transformers: Revenge of the Fallen."
- The Wadi Mujib Nature Reserve in Jordan is home to a breathtaking canyon known as the "Grand Canyon of Jordan."
- The Jordanian dessert called "Knafeh" is a popular sweet made of shredded filo pastry, cheese, and sweet syrup.
- Jordan has a rich history of traditional arts and crafts, including calligraphy, weaving, and silver jewelry making.

CHOOSE THE CORRECT OPTION ABOUT JORDAN

1. **What is the national animal of Jordan?**
   - a) Arabian Horse b) Arabian Oryx c) Arabian Leopard
2. **What is the national bird of Jordan?**
   - a) Sinai Rosefinch b) Arabian Falcon c) Jordanian Sparrow
3. **What is the national sport of Jordan?**
   - a) Basketball b) Football (Soccer) c) Swimming
4. **Which tree is the national tree of Jordan?**
   - a) Palm Tree b) Oak Tree c) Olive Tree
5. **What is the official name of Jordan?**
   - a) Kingdom of Jordan b) Republic of Jordan c) Hashemite Kingdom of Jordan
6. **How many provinces is Jordan divided into?**
   - a) 6 provinces b) 10 provinces c) 12 provinces
7. **What percentage of the world's land does Jordan occupy?**
   - a) 0.1% b) 0.3% c) 1%
8. **In which months are the coldest months in Jordan?**
   - a) March, April, May b) June, July, August c) December, January, February
9. **In which months are the hottest months in Jordan?**
   - a) September, October b) July, August c) November, December
10. **What was the old name of Jordan?**
    - a) Jordanian Kingdom b) Hashemite Empire c) Transjordan
11. **What is the national nickname of Jordan?**
    - a) Land of Deserts b) The Hashemite Kingdom c) Land of Ancient Ruins
12. **Who was the first ruler of Jordan?**
    - a) King Hussein b) Emir Abdullah I c) King Abdullah II

Answer Key:

1. b) Arabian Oryx
2. a) Sinai Rosefinch
3. b) Football (Soccer)
4. b) Oak Tree
5. c) Hashemite Kingdom of Jordan
6. c) 12 provinces
7. b) 0.3%
8. c) December, January, February
9. b) July, August
10. c) Transjordan
11. b) The Hashemite Kingdom
12. b) Emir Abdullah I

Made in the USA
Las Vegas, NV
05 December 2024